Contents

Meets Accreditation Standard for Child-created Bulletin Boards

Three Cheers for September PreK–K, SV 9828-0

Introduction

This series of monthly activity books is designed to give PreK and Kindergarten teachers a collection of hands-on activities and ideas for each month of the year. The activities are standards-based and reflect the philosophy that children learn best through play. The teacher can use these ideas to enhance the development of language and math skills, and of social/emotional and physical growth of children. The opportunity to promote pre-reading skills is present throughout the series and should be incorporated whenever possible.

Organization and Features

Each book consists of seven units:

Unit 1 provides reproducible pages and information for the month in general.
- a newsletter outline to promote parent communication
- a blank thematic border page
- a list of special days in the month
- calendar ideas to promote math skills
- a blank calendar grid that can also be used as an incentive chart

Units 2–6 include an array of activities for five theme topics. Each unit includes
- teacher information on the theme
- arts and crafts ideas
- a food activity
- poetry, songs, and books
- bulletin board ideas
- center activities correlated to specific learning standards

Implement the activities in a way that best meets the needs of individual children.

Unit 7 focuses on a well-known **children's author**. The unit includes
- a biography of the author
- activities based on a literature selection
- a list of books by the author
- reproducible bookmarks

In addition, each book contains
- reproducible icons suitable to use as labels for centers in the classroom. The icons coordinate with the centers in the book. They may also be used with a work assignment chart to aid in assigning children to centers.
- reproducible **student awards**
- a **calendar day pattern** with suggested activities

Research Base

Howard Gardner's theory of multiple intelligences, or learning styles, validates teaching thematically and using a variety of approaches to help children learn. Providing a variety of experiences will assure that each child has an opportunity to learn in a comfortable way.

Following are the learning styles identified by Howard Gardner.
- **Verbal/Linguistic** learners need opportunities to read, listen, write, learn new words, and tell stories.
- **Bodily/Kinesthetic** learners learn best through physical activities.
- **Musical** learners enjoy music activities.
- **Logical/Mathematical** learners need opportunities to problem solve, count, measure, and do patterning activities.
- **Visual/Spatial** learners need opportunities to paint, draw, sculpt, and create artworks.
- **Interpersonal** learners benefit from group discussions and group projects.
- **Intrapersonal** learners learn best in solitary activities, such as reading, writing in journals, and reflecting on information.
- **Naturalist** learners need opportunities to observe weather and nature and to take care of animals and plants.
- **Existential** learners can be fostered in the early years by asking children to think and respond, by discussions, and by writing.

Gardner, H. (1994). *Frames of mind*. New York: Basic Books.

September News

Teacher:_____ Date:_____

Headline News

Coming Up

Happy Birthday to

Special Thanks to

Help Wanted

September

Special Days in September

National Library Month Have children dictate a chart-sized thank-you letter to the local librarian and draw pictures from their favorite books. Then arrange a trip to the local library so children can take their pictures and letter.

Children's Good Manners Month Read *The Berenstain Bears Forget Their Manners* by Stan and Jan Berenstain. Then discuss the importance of good manners in school.

Labor Day Labor Day is the first Monday in September. Have children celebrate with activities from the Helpers in Our Neighborhood unit that begins on page 55.

Grandparent's Day This day is the first Sunday after Labor Day. Celebrate by inviting the children's grandparents to story and snack time.

8 Jack Prelutsky's Birthday Read some poems by Jack Prelutsky in honor of his birthday.

9 Teddy Bear Day Have children bring a favorite stuffed bear to class and read a bear story aloud to them.

11 Patriot Day Discuss the meaning of *patriot*. Then point out an American flag. Discuss the colors and patterns children see. Then talk about the meaning of the flag.

16 Collect Rocks Day Take children on a walk around the school grounds and invite them to find one interesting rock. Provide art supplies for them to make a rock creature.

17 National Apple Dumpling Day Have children flatten an uncooked biscuit and scoop a spoonful of apple-pie filling on one half of it. Help them fold the dough and seal it. Bake the "dumpling" according to directions and eat the treat for snack.

19 National Butterscotch Pudding Day Have children help make butterscotch pudding and eat it for snack.

21 or 22 Fall Take the children on a walk around the school and point out signs of fall. Invite children to draw a picture of something they saw. Then help them dictate a sentence to go along with their picture.

22 National Dear Diary Day Choose a book that is written in a diary format and read it to children. Then have them dictate a diary letter about something they have done during the day.

26 Johnny Appleseed Day Have children celebrate with activities from the Apples, Apples, Apples unit that begins on page 70.

Three Cheers for September PreK–K, SV 9828-0

September

Sunday	Monday	Tuesday	Wednesday	Thursday	Friday	Saturday

Three Cheers for September PreK–K, SV 9828-0

Calendar Activities for September

Classroom Calendar Setup

The use of the calendar in the classroom can provide children with daily practice in learning days, weeks, months, and years. As you plan the setup for your classroom, include enough space on the wall to staple a calendar grid labeled with the days of the week. Leave space above the grid for the name of the month and the year. Next to the calendar, staple twelve cards labeled with the months of the year and the number of days in each month. Leave these items on the wall all year. At the beginning of each month, start with the blank calendar grid. Do not staple anything on the grid that refers to the new month. Leave the days of the week and the year in place.

Introducing the Month of September

Before children arrive, gather all of the items that will go on the calendar for September. You may want to include the following:

- name of the month
- number cards
- name cards to indicate birthdays during the month
- picture cards that tell about special holidays or school events during the month
- a small treat to be taped on the day of each child's birthday. You may wish to gift-wrap the treat.

Add a special pointer that can be used each day while doing calendar activities. See page 9 for directions on how to make a pointer. Place these items in a picnic basket. Select a puppet that can remain in the basket and come out only to bring items for each new month. A dog puppet works well because of the large mouth, which makes it easier to grasp each item.

On the first school day of the month, follow this procedure:

1. Place the picnic basket in front of the class. Pull out the puppet and introduce it to children if it is the first time they have seen it or ask them if they remember why the puppet is here. If this is the first time they have seen it, explain that the puppet will visit on the first day of each month to bring the new calendar items.

2. Have the puppet pull out the name of the month. According to the abilities of children, have them name the first letter in the name of the month, count the letters, or find the vowels. Staple the name of the month above the calendar.

3. Have the puppet pull out the new pointer for the teacher or the daily helper to use each day during calendar time.

4. Next, pull out the number cards for September. You may use plain number cards, cards made from the calendar day pattern on page 96, or seasonal die-cut shapes. By using two or three die-cut shapes, you can incorporate building patterns as part of your daily calendar routine. See page 9 for pattern ideas.

Three Cheers for September PreK–K, SV 9828-0

5. Place the number one card or die-cut under the day of the week on which September begins. Locate September on the month cards that are stapled next to your calendar. Have children tell how many days this month will have and then count that many spaces on the calendar to indicate the end of the month. You may wish to place a small stop sign as a visual reminder of the end of the month. Save the remaining numbers cards or die-cut shapes and add one each day.

6. If there are any birthdays during September, have the puppet pull out of the basket the cards that have a birthday symbol with the child's name and birth date written on it. Count from the number 1 to find where to staple these as a visual reminder of each child's birthday. If you have included a wrapped treat for each child, tape it on the calendar on the correct day.

7. Finally, have the puppet bring out cards that have pictures of holidays or special happenings, such as field trips, picture day, or story time in the library. Staple the picture cards on the correct day on the calendar grid. You can use these to practice various counting skills such as counting how many days until a field trip, a birthday, or a holiday.

8. When the basket is empty, say goodbye to the puppet and return it to the picnic basket. Put the basket away until the next month. Children will look forward to the beginning of each month in order to see what items the puppet will bring for the class calendar.

Making an Apple Pointer

Include an apple pointer in the calendar basket for this month. To make a pointer, you will need the following:

- two 3" apple shapes cut from poster board
- a medium-sized dowel rod that is 18" long
- several 12" lengths of narrow red and yellow ribbon

Directions:

1. Hot-glue the ribbons to the end of the dowel rod so that they lie against the rod.
2. Hot-glue the two apple shapes to the end of the dowel rod so that the apples cover the glued ends of the ribbons.

The calendar helper can use this to point to the day of the week, the number, the month, and the year as the class says the date each day.

Developing a Pattern

Practice the concept of patterning by writing the numbers 1–30 on two die-cut shapes, such as an apple and a fall leaf. Write the numbers on the shapes in the order using an ABABAB pattern. After the first few days, ask the children if they notice anything special about the shapes on the calendar. Younger children may not understand patterning yet but will become more aware as the pattern develops.

Feeling Good Facts

 People use 26 muscles to smile and 62 muscles to frown.

 Smiling actually promotes the nervous system to produce a chemical that gives a pleasant feeling to the whole body. Likewise, a frown often causes increased blood flow to the feet and hands, a sign of anger.

 The most famous smile is a painting of a Florence lady—Lisa. Leonardo da Vinci painted *Mona Lisa* between 1503 and 1506. It is an oil painting that is about 30 x 21 inches.

 Stress can affect the emotional state of a person and lead to physical health problems as well.

 There is a direct correlation between exercise and mental health—exercise increases the production of chemicals that cause happiness and a positive sense of well-being.

 Newborn babies have 300 bones. As people grow, some of the bones fuse together to give humans a total of 206 bones.

 People grow until around the age of 20. They remain at that height until nearly 50 years old, at which time there is a gradual decline in height.

 Heredity is the passing down of physical and mental traits from parent to child. Some traits include eye and hair color. One interesting trait is the ability of a person to roll the tongue. A person can either do this "trick" or not.

Face Puppets

Materials

- small paper plates
- craft sticks
- yarn that matches hair colors
- markers
- glue
- scissors

Directions

Teacher Preparation: Choose yarn to match the color of the child's hair. Cut the yarn into pieces to make hair.

1. Draw a happy face on the inside of one plate.
2. Draw a sad face on the inside of the second plate.
3. Glue yarn hair around both plates.
4. Glue the plates back-to-back on one end of a craft stick. Set aside to dry.

After the puppets are dry, discuss with children different situations in which they are happy or sad. Have them hold up their puppets to show the feeling they would experience.

Life-size Me

Materials

- mural paper
- markers
- crayons
- scissors

Directions

Teacher Preparation: Cut mural paper into five-foot long lengths. Invite parent helpers to class on the designated day. Then have children take turns lying on the paper and tracing the outlines of each other's bodies.

1. Draw facial features and clothes on the paper doll to look like you.
2. Cut around the outline of the doll.

Unit 2, Me and My Feelings: Arts and Crafts
Three Cheers for September PreK–K, SV 9828-0

Pizza Person

You will need

- canned biscuits
- pizza sauce
- baking trays
- mozzarella cheese
- olives
- green pepper
- pepperoni
- foil
- spoons
- knife
- grater
- scissors

Directions

Teacher Preparation: Cut the foil into squares so that each child will have one. Slice the toppings into different sizes and shapes so that children can be creative in making the facial features on their pizzas. You may wish to invite children to help grate the cheese. Place each ingredient in its own bowl with a spoon. Bake the pizzas in a 375°F oven until they are lightly brown.

1. Flatten a biscuit on a foil square to make the pizza crust.

2. Spread sauce over the crust.

3. Sprinkle cheese on the pizza for hair.

4. Choose ingredients to make the eyes, ears, nose, and mouth.

5. Place the foil on a baking tray.

Note: Be aware of children who may have food allergies.

Me

(Have children point to each body part as it is named.)

I have ten tiny fingers

And ten tiny toes,

Two tiny arms

And one tiny nose.

One tiny mouth

And two tiny ears,

Two tiny eyes

For smiles and tears.

One tiny head

And two tiny feet,

One tiny chin—

That's ME!

I'm complete!

Me Books

Feelings
by Aliki (Dimensions)

The Feelings Box
by Ronald M. Gold (Aegina Press)

I'm Gonna Like Me: Letting Off a Little Self-Esteem
by Jamie Lee Curtis (Joanna Cotler)

Me and My Amazing Body
by Joan Sweeney (Dragonfly)

My First Body Book
by Christopher Rice (DK Publishing)

My Own Human Body
by Giovanni Caviezel (Barron's Educational Series)

Today I Feel Silly: And Other Moods That Make My Day
by Jamie Lee Curtis (Joanna Cotler)

The Way I Feel
by Janan Cain (Parenting Press)

When Sophie Gets Angry—Really, Really Angry
by Molly Bang (Scholastic)

I Am Special

Look in the mirror.
What do I see?
Someone
who's special-

**Wow!
I see me!**

Materials

- large unbreakable mirror (or several smaller ones)
- thumbtacks
- blue craft paper
- border
- lunch bags
- children's pictures
- recycled magazines
- scissors
- glue
- stapler

Directions

Teacher Preparation: Cover the board with the craft paper. Use thumbtacks to secure the mirror to the board. Write the poem above the mirror. Send a letter home with children asking parents or guardians to help their child pick out a favorite toy or something special to share at show and tell. Ask children to enclose it in a bag to keep the item a secret. Add a border and the caption to the bulletin board.

1. Look through magazines and cut out pictures of things that you like to do or that show things about you, such as a favorite color or food.

2. Glue the cutouts or draw pictures on the outside of a bag.

3. Glue your picture to the bag.

Open the bag and help children staple it to the bulletin board. Have them put their item inside the bag. During show and tell time, allow each child to look in the mirror and recite the poem. Then have the child share his or her bag, telling what makes the child special.

Three Cheers for September PreK–K, SV 9828-0

Learning About Me Centers

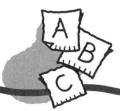

Language Center

Language Arts Standard
Writes own name legibly and correctly

Namely Me

Materials

- activity master on page 19
- contact paper or laminate
- washable markers
- paper towels
- sentence strips
- markers
- water-filled spray bottle

Teacher Preparation: Write each child's first name on a sentence strip. Cover the strips with contact paper or laminate them. Duplicate the activity master for each child. Demonstrate for children how to clean the sentence strip by lightly spraying the water on the strip and wiping it with paper towels.

Invite children to practice tracing the letters in their names. When they are comfortable with writing, have them write their names on the activity master and circle the letters in the alphabet that make up their names.

Art Center

Math Standard
Applies and adapts a variety of strategies to solve problems

Self-portraits

Materials

- easel
- large paper
- tempera paints
- unbreakable mirror

Teacher Preparation: Hang the mirror next to the easel at the child's eye level.

Explain that a self-portrait is a picture that an artist paints of himself or herself. Then invite children to paint a self-portrait. Encourage them to look in the mirror as they paint.

Learning About Me Centers

Language Center

Language Arts Standard
Begins to respond to oral presentations based on personal experience as a listener and speaker

Emotional Interview

Materials

- patterns on pages 20 and 21
- tape recorder
- contact paper or laminate
- white construction paper
- cassette tape
- markers

Teacher Preparation: Duplicate one copy of each page of the "Faces of Feelings" patterns on white paper. Color the faces and cover them with contact paper or laminate them.

Name each feeling on the pages and invite children to share times they have felt those feelings. Then invite children to work with a partner and take turns interviewing and recording each other about times when they have experienced one of the emotions. Remind them to say their names as they record each other.

Game Center

Math Standard
Creates and interprets visuals including pictures and maps

Feeling a Match

Materials

- patterns on pages 20 and 21
- file folders
- markers
- glue
- white construction paper
- envelopes
- scissors

Teacher Preparation: Duplicate two copies of each page of the "Faces of Feelings" patterns on white paper. Color the faces, cut them out, and glue one set of eight pictures on the inside of a file folder. You may wish to make several file folders. Laminate the folders and the remaining loose faces. Store the loose faces in an envelope.

Have children match the faces and identify the feelings.

Learning About Me Centers

Science Center

Science Standard
Understands characteristics of organisms

My Own Print

Materials

- activity master on page 22
- paper
- wipes
- ink pad
- hand lenses
- crayons

Teacher Preparation: Duplicate the "Fingerprint Shapes" activity master for each child.

Explain that every person has his or her own special set of fingerprints. Then invite children to make a print of their fingers on the activity master. Have them use a hand lens to look at their own prints and compare them to the shapes on the activity master. Then have them compare their own prints to the prints of the other members in the center.

Math Center

Math Standard
Creates and interprets a simple graph that uses pictures

Graphing Names

Materials

- magnetic letters
- small paper plates
- craft paper
- marker
- metal baking trays
- tape

Teacher Preparation: Make a pictograph on craft paper. Lines should be about eight inches apart, or the width of a small plate. Write numbers from 1 to 10, or more if children's names have more than ten letters. Label the pictograph "Letters in Our Names." You may wish to place the sentence strips with children's names completed in "Namely Me" on page 15 in the center for those children assigned to this center.

Have children use the magnetic letters to spell their names on the baking sheets. Then have them draw a picture of themselves on a plate and write their names around the edge. Ask children to count the letters in their names, find the corresponding number on the pictograph, and tape it on that row. When each child has completed the activity, discuss the purpose of the graph and help children read it.

Learning About Me Centers

Dramatic Play Center

Social Studies Standard
Creates and interprets visuals including pictures and maps

Name That Feeling

Materials

- pattern on page 23
- crayons
- clear tape
- white construction paper
- scissors
- glue

Teacher Preparation: Duplicate the cube pattern on white paper. Draw and color a face showing a different emotion on each of the six squares. Cut out the cube, fold it on the lines, and glue it as indicated. Tape the edges to make the cube stronger.

Invite children to take turns rolling the cube. Have them identify the emotion that it lands on and make movements and expressions that pantomime the emotion.

Block Center

Math Standard
Measures length using nonstandard materials

As Tall as Me

Materials

- activity master on page 24
- paper dolls (completed in "Life-size Me" on page 11)
- blocks

Teacher Preparation: Duplicate the "How Tall?" activity master for each child.

Ask children to use different kinds of blocks to find out how tall they are. Challenge them to estimate, or guess, first and then find the actual measurement by laying the blocks end-to-end beside their paper dolls.

Name _____

Letters in My Name

A B C D E F
G H I J K L M
N O P Q R S T
U V W X Y Z

a b c d e f
g h i j k l m
n o p q r s t
u v w x y z

Directions: Use with "Namely Me" on page 15. Have children write their names and circle the letters in the alphabet that make up their names.

Unit 2, Me and My Feelings: Activity Master
Three Cheers for September PreK–K, SV 9828-0

Faces of Feelings Patterns

Use with "Emotional Interview" and "Feeling a Match" on page 16.

happy

angry

afraid

silly

Faces of Feelings Patterns

Use with "Emotional Interview" and "Feeling a Match" on page 16.

sad

surprised

worried

loving

Three Cheers for September PreK–K, SV 9828-0

Name _____

Fingerprint Shapes

whorls

loops

arches

Directions: Use with "My Own Print" on page 17. Invite children to make a print of their fingers on the activity master. Have them use a hand lens to look at their own prints and compare them to the shapes on the activity master. Then have them compare their own prints to the prints of the other members in the center.

Feelings Cube Pattern

Use with "Name That Feeling" on page 18.

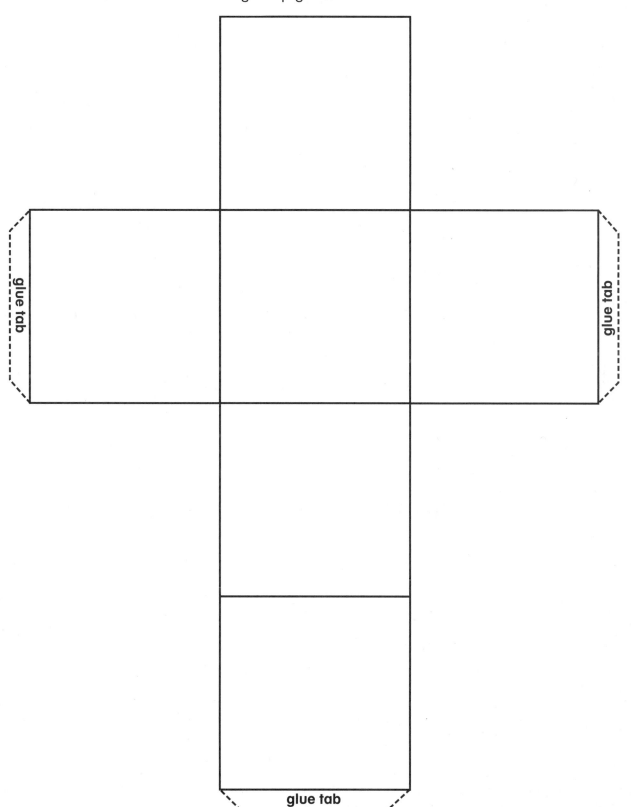

glue tab

glue tab

glue tab

Three Cheers for September PreK–K, SV 9828-0

How Tall?

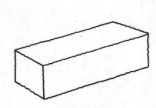

Estimate: _____

Measure: _____

Estimate: _____

Measure: _____

Estimate: _____

Measure: _____

Directions: Use with "As Tall as Me" on page 18. Have children use different kinds of blocks to find out how tall they are. Challenge them to estimate, or guess, first and then find the actual measurement by laying the blocks end-to-end beside their paper dolls.

Color Notes

 Scientists estimate there may be over ten million colors.

 There are seven colors of light in a rainbow: red, orange, yellow, green, blue, indigo, and violet. They always are in the same order.

 A rainbow is made when millions of raindrops bend light. When the light bends, the seven colors can be seen in light.

 The primary colors are red, blue, and yellow. They can be mixed together to create any other color. Primary colors cannot be made from other colors.

 The secondary colors are green (yellow + blue), orange (yellow + red), and purple (blue + red). A secondary color is made by mixing two primary colors.

 The first box of crayons was developed in 1903 and had eight colors.

 When children work in a yellow environment, their performance seems to improve.

 Long ago, artists made paint colors with items they found in nature. Onionskins were used to make yellow, and plant leaves were used to make green.

 Colors often have emotional meanings. Blue means "sad," green means "jealous," and red means "angry."

 Most bubble gum is pink. This color was chosen originally because it was the only color that the gum inventor had.

Three Cheers for September PreK–K, SV 9828-0

Glued on Color

Materials

- bottles of white glue
- tempera paints
- white construction paper
- markers or crayons

Directions

Teacher Preparation: Make sure bottles are two-thirds full of white glue. Add a color of tempera paint to fill each bottle. Shake the bottles to mix the glue and paint.

1. Use the different colors of glue to draw the outline of a picture.

2. Set the picture aside to dry.

3. Use markers or crayons in matching colors to finish coloring the picture.

Colorful Sun Catcher

Materials

- tissue paper in a variety of colors
- large plastic lids (coffee or whipped topping)
- glue
- water
- paintbrushes
- containers and bowls
- scissors
- tape

Directions

Teacher Preparation: Cut the tissue paper into squares. Place each color in its own container or bowl. Mix equal amounts of water and glue in a bowl. Put a paintbrush in the glue mixture.

1. Paint a layer of glue on the surface of a plastic lid.

2. Lay different colors of tissue-paper squares on the glue. Be sure to overlap the squares. Notice the new colors that form.

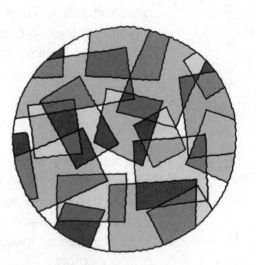

3. When the entire lid is covered with tissue paper, paint more glue on the surface to seal the tissue paper.

4. Set the lid aside to dry.

5. Trim paper that hangs over the edges so that the sun catcher is the shape of a circle.

6. Pull the dried paper off the lid.

7. Tape the sun catcher on a window to see the different colors.

Three Cheers for September PreK–K, SV 9828-0

Rainbow Yogurt

You will need

- red, orange, yellow, green, blue, purple, and pink sugar-free gelatin mix
- vanilla yogurt
- large paper plates
- cups
- spoons

Directions

Teacher Preparation: Pour each color of gelatin mix in its own cup. Set a spoon in each cup.

1. Spoon the yogurt onto the plate and spread it out to cover the bottom.

2. Sprinkle a thin band of each color of gelatin across the yogurt to look like a rainbow.

Note: Be aware of children who may have food allergies.

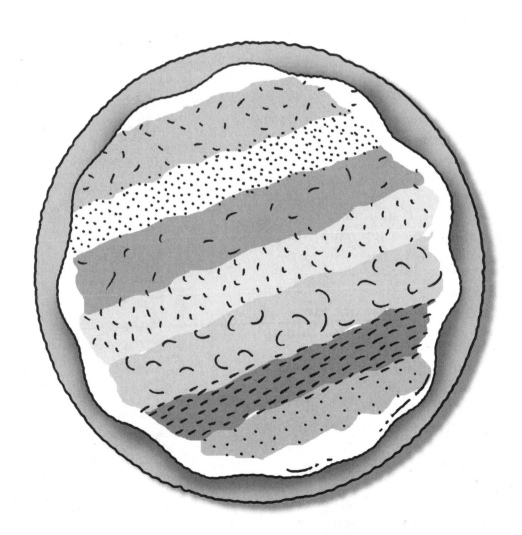

Three Cheers for September PreK–K, SV 9828-0

♫ Color Chant

Teacher Preparation: Make a chart of the chant, writing the color words in the corresponding marker color. Then enlarge, duplicate, and cut out the pictures on page 34. Color them to match the song. Invite volunteers to attach the pictures with sticky adhesive to the chart as they chant.

Colors, colors,
Oh, so bright!
Follow along with all your might!
(Clap, clap, stomp—Clap, clap, stomp)

Red is an apple.
Red is a rose.
Spin around and touch your toes.
(Clap, clap, stomp—Clap, clap, stomp)

Orange is a pumpkin.
Orange is a carrot.
Echo me like you're a parrot!
(Clap, clap, stomp—Clap, clap, stomp)

Yellow is a pear.
Yellow is the sun.
Tap your head—now we're havin' fun!
(Clap, clap, stomp—Clap, clap, stomp)

Green is grass.
Green is a pea.
Wiggle all about, if you please.
(Clap, clap, stomp—Clap, clap, stomp)

Blue is the sky.
Blue is the sea.
Jump up and down, just like me.
(Clap, clap, stomp—Clap, clap, stomp)

Brown is chocolate.
Brown is sand.
Show me your fingers and wiggle your hands.
(Clap, clap, stomp—Clap, clap, stomp)

Black is licorice.
Black is night.
Thanks for chanting with all your might!
(Clap, clap, stomp—Clap, clap, stomp)

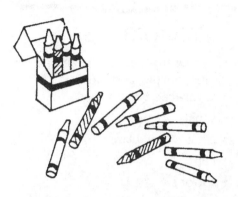

Beautiful Reading Books

Brown Bear, Brown Bear, What Do You See?
by Bill Martin (Henry Holt and Co.)

The Crayon Box That Talked
by Shane Derolf and Michael Letzig (Random House)

Color Dance
by Ann Jonas (Greenwillow)

Colors All Around
by Gail Gibbons (Holiday House)

Color Surprises
by Chuck Murphy (Little Simon)

Mary Wore Her Red Dress
by Merle Peek (Houghton Mifflin)

Little Blue and Little Yellow
by Leo Lionni (HarperTrophy)

Mouse Paint
by Ellen Stoll (Voyager)

Planting a Rainbow
by Lois Ehlert (Voyager Books)

Three Cheers for September PreK–K, SV 9828-0

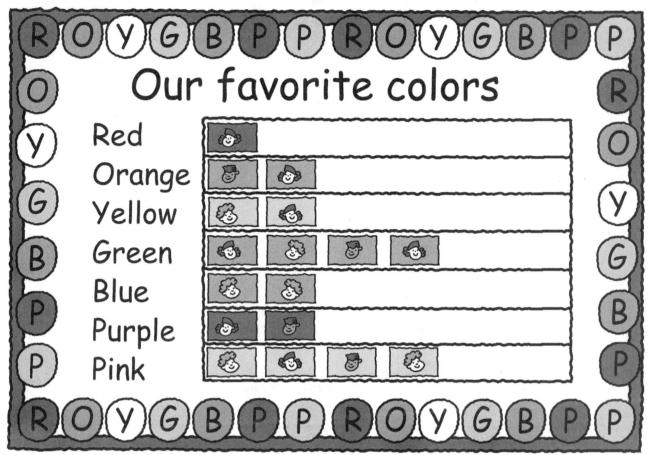

Materials

- red, orange, yellow, green, blue, purple, pink construction paper
- white craft paper
- permanent marker
- markers
- stapler
- scissors

Directions

Teacher Preparation: Cover the bulletin board with white paper. Draw a graph with seven rows using a permanent marker. Label each row with a color word, writing the word in the same color marker. Cut out circles of each color of paper to make a patterned border. Create a repeated color pattern across the top of the board to begin the border. Finally, cut several pieces of each color of construction paper in half.

1. Choose your favorite color of construction paper.

2. Draw a picture of yourself on the paper and write your name on the back.

Have children name their favorite color. Then help them match the color to the word and staple their picture in the corresponding row to make a bar graph. Have them identify the color pattern of the border and name the next color circle to add to it. Staple the color in place. Once the graph and border are complete, ask simple questions about the graph data, such as: *What color do the most children like? Which color do the least number of children like?*

Color Centers

Math Center

Color by Number

Materials

- patterns on page 35
- white construction paper
- scissors
- activity master on page 36
- crayons
- glue

Teacher Preparation: Duplicate the activity master for each child. Duplicate one copy of the crayon patterns. Color the crayons, cut them out, and glue them to another sheet of construction paper to make the coloring code shown.

Have children follow the code to color the picture on the activity master.

red	= 1
green	= 2
purple	= 3
orange	= 4
blue	= 5

Language Center

Color Rhymes

Materials

- patterns on page 35
- white construction paper
- scissors
- cards on page 37
- crayons
- glue

Teacher Preparation: Duplicate one copy of the crayon patterns and one copy of the picture cards. Color and cut out the red, green, blue, pink, brown, and black crayons. Color and cut apart the picture cards. Cut a sheet of paper into rectangles that are the same size as the picture cards. Glue a crayon on each rectangle to make crayon picture cards.

Review the picture names and color names shown on the cards. Then invite children to match pictures and colors whose names rhyme.

Color Centers

Game Center

Math Standard
Sorts and classifies by size, color, shape, or kind

Beanbag Colors

Materials

- construction paper in a variety of colors
- scrap paper
- beanbags
- tape
- crayons

Teacher Preparation: Tape one of each color of construction paper on the floor. Make a tape line four feet from the construction paper. Set three beanbags behind the tape line.

Invite children to take turns standing behind the tape line and tossing the beanbags to play two different games. Have a child call out a color. A partner tries to throw a beanbag on that color. Children also can toss a beanbag and name the color it lands on. If the child names the correct color, he or she gets a point. The first player to reach ten points wins.

Block Center

Math Standard
Sorts and classifies by size, color, shape, or kind

Block Pictures

Materials

- color shape blocks

Invite children to use the blocks to make colorful pictures. Ask them to describe the block shapes and colors they used when the pictures are complete.

Color Centers

Sensory Center

Language Arts Standard
Gives and receives feedback by sharing and speaking with others

Colorful Scents

Materials

- sugar-free gelatin
- cream of tartar
- saucepan
- containers with lids or resealable plastic bags
- flour
- boiling water
- spoon
- measuring cup
- salt
- cooking oil
- measuring spoons
- wax paper

Teacher Preparation: You may wish to make several colors of dough for children to experience. For each dough recipe, mix together 0.3 ounces of gelatin, 2 cups of flour, I cup of salt, and 4 tablespoons of cream of tartar in a saucepan. Add 2 cups of boiling water and 2 tablespoons of oil and stir over medium heat until the mixture forms a ball. Cool the dough on wax paper.

Invite children to smell the dough and name the flavor. Ask them what color the dough is. Then challenge children to make shapes of things that are the same color as the dough.

Science Center

Science Standard
Performs experiments with materials to notice change

Color Mixing

Materials

- coffee filters
- spray bottle
- markers
- newspaper
- water
- paper towels

Teacher Preparation: Fill the bottle with water. Cover the table with newspaper.

Invite children to draw shapes or scribble with markers on a coffee filter. Then ask them to put the filter on a paper towel. Have children lightly spray water on the filter. Ask them to describe the new colors that form when the colors bleed together.

Color Centers

Writing Center

Language Arts Standard
Uses letters to represent words

Color Booklet

Materials

- activity masters on pages 38 and 39
- stapler
- crayons
- construction paper
- pencils

Teacher Preparation: Duplicate the booklet pages. Make a cover from construction paper and assemble the books. Provide a copy for each child.

Read each color word as children follow along in the booklet. Help them identify the picture names. Have them trace each color word using the corresponding color of crayon and color the things on the page that are that color.

Music Center

Language Arts Standard
Gives and receives feedback by sharing and speaking with others

More Color Chanting

Materials

- chart completed for "Color Chant" on page 28
- patterns on page 34 completed for "Color Chant" on page 28

Invite children to hold up the correct pictures as they say the chant.

Color Chant Pieces Patterns

Use with "Color Chant" on page 28 and "More Color Chanting" on page 33.

apple

rose

pumpkin

carrot

grass

pear

pea

licorice

sea

sun

chocolate

sky

sand

night

Three Cheers for September PreK–K, SV 9828-0

Crayon Patterns

Use with "Color by Number" and "Color Rhymes" on page 30.

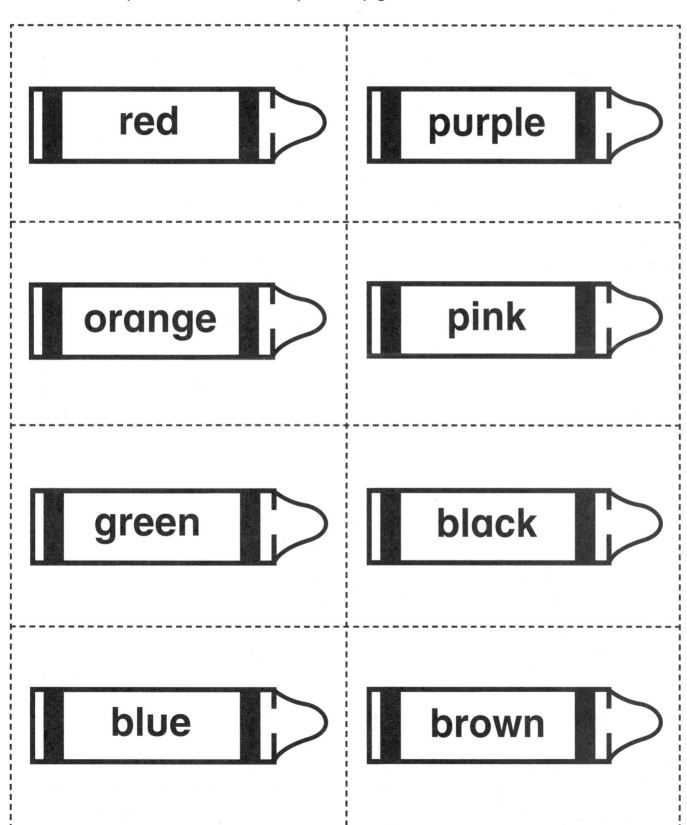

red

purple

orange

pink

green

black

blue

brown

Name

Hidden Picture

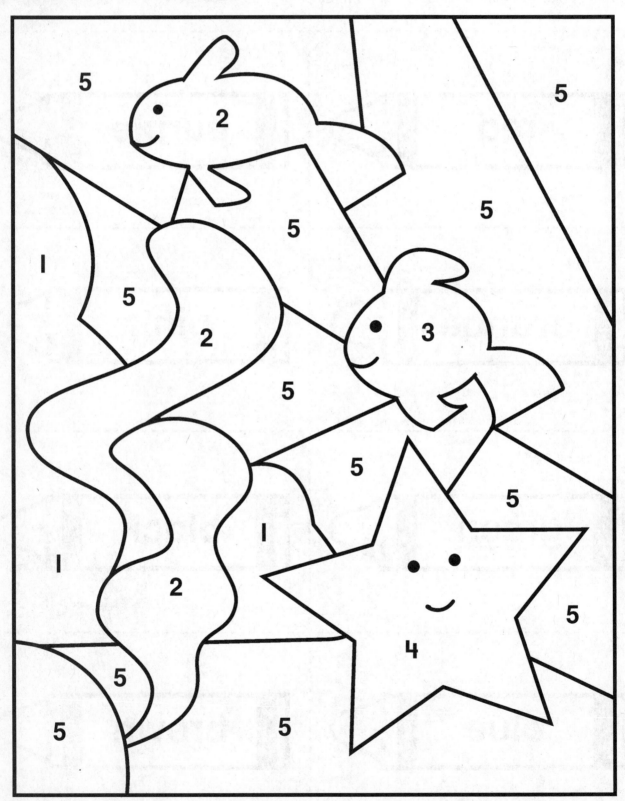

Directions: Use with "Color by Number" on page 30. Have children follow the code to color the picture.

Unit 3, Colors All Around: Activity Master
Three Cheers for September PreK–K, SV 9828-0

Rhyming Picture Cards

Use with "Color Rhymes" on page 30.

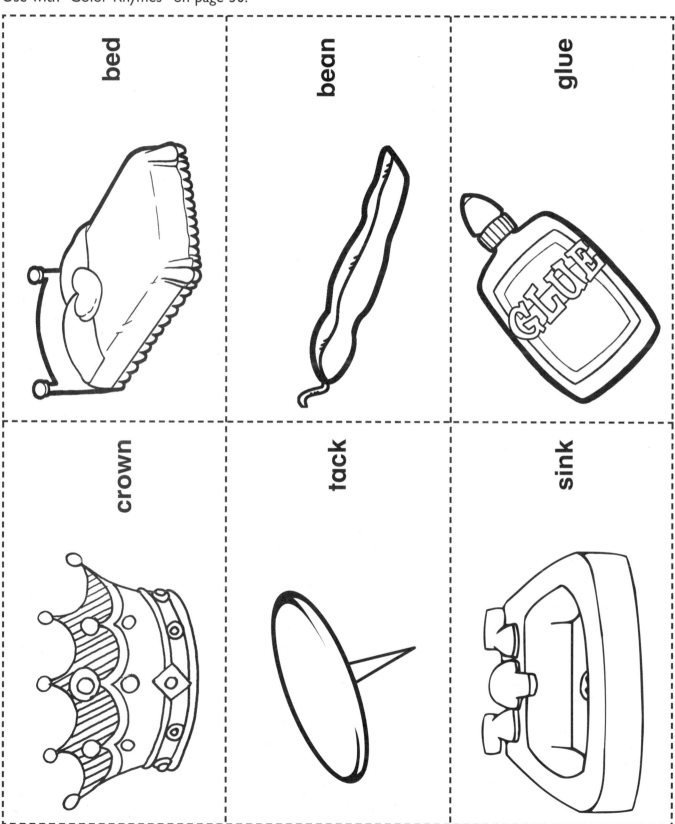

| bed | bean | glue |
| crown | tack | sink |

Three Cheers for September PreK–K, SV 9828-0

Color Booklet

Use with "Color Booklet" on page 33.

red

1

blue

2

   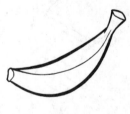

yellow

3

Unit 3, Colors All Around: Activity Master
Three Cheers for September PreK–K, SV 9828-0

Color Booklet

Use with "Color Booklet" on page 33.

_____

green

4

_____

orange

5

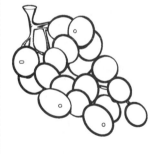   

_____

purple

6

Unit 3, Colors All Around: Activity Master
Three Cheers for September PreK–K, SV 9828-0

Mother Goose News

 A nursery rhyme is a poem with rhythm and rhyme often used to amuse or soothe young children. It is a form of folk literature passed down by word of mouth.

 There was no such person as Mother Goose. The name first appeared in 1650 in France when a writer used the phrase "like a Mother Goose story." The name really took hold nearly 50 years later when a picture of an old woman telling stories appeared on the cover of a book. There was a sign on the cover that read "Tales of My Mother the Goose."

 Mother Goose Day is May 1.

 Some of the well-loved nursery rhymes, such as "Rock-a-by Baby," began as ballads for adults. They were watered down over the years and became acceptable for children.

 Some nursery rhymes were teaching songs for the alphabet and counting.

 Some nursery rhymes were used as tickle games, such as "To Market, To Market," for infants and toddlers.

 Some rhymes refer to historical events. For example, "Ring Around the Rosie" may have been written around the time of the plague in London. "Ashes! Ashes! We all fall down" refers to the people who had died.

 Many rhymes were social comments and protests about historical events, such as "Baa, Baa Black Sheep," which referred to the English exporting tax in the 1200's.

 So what was Miss Muffet really eating? Curds are the thick parts of milk that separate from the watery part of milk when it curdles. Cheese is made from the curds of milk.

 A tuffet is a low stool or seat.

 The muffin man worked on Drury Lane. Drury Lane is a street in central London made famous when a theater was built in 1662. The theater still exists today, after being rebuilt four different times.

Hickory, Dickory, Clock

Materials

- patterns on page 49
- construction paper
- craft sticks
- crayons
- glue
- scissors
- straightedge blade (optional)

Directions

Teacher Preparation: Duplicate a clock and mouse on construction paper for each child. You may want to use a straightedge blade to cut the slit for children.

1. Color the clock and mouse.
2. Cut out the clock and mouse.
3. Glue the clock on a piece of construction paper.
4. Ask a teacher to help you cut the slit.
5. Glue the mouse on one end of a stick.
6. When the mouse is dry, push the mouse through the slit and repeat the "Hickory, Dickory, Dock" rhyme.

Kitten Mitten

Materials

- pattern on page 50
- white construction paper
- large paper clips
- hole punch
- yarn
- crayons or markers
- scissors

Directions

Teacher Preparation: Duplicate two mitten patterns for each child. Cut the yarn into two-yard lengths.

1. Place two mittens facedown on the table with the thumbs side-by-side.
2. Color the mittens so they look alike.
3. Cut out the mittens.
4. Stack and paper clip the mittens together.
5. Punch holes as shown on the pattern.
6. Sew the mittens together with yarn.
7. Repeat the "Three Little Kittens" rhyme.

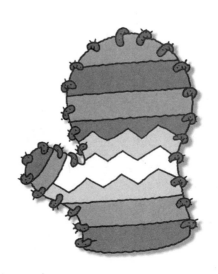

Three Cheers for September PreK–K, SV 9828-0

Humpty-Dumpty Bread

You will need

- eggs
- bread
- plastic cups
- biscuit cutter (optional)
- spray shortening
- salt
- pepper
- electric skillet with lid
- spatula
- paper plates
- forks

Directions

1. Use a cup or biscuit cutter to cut a hole in the center of a slice of bread.

2. Crack an egg into a cup.

3. Ask an adult to place the bread in the skillet to toast.

4. When lightly browned, flip the bread over.

5. Pour the egg into the hole of the bread.

6. Add salt and pepper if desired.

7. Cover the skillet and cook until the egg is done.

Note: Be aware of children who may have food allergies.

♫ Music and Movement

The following rhymes are used in this unit.

Three Little Kittens

Three little kittens
Lost their mittens,
And they began to cry,
Oh, Mother dear, we sadly fear
Our mittens we have lost.

What? Lost your mittens,
You naughty kittens!
Then you shall have no pie.
Mee-ow, mee-ow, mee-ow,
No, you shall have no pie!

Hickory, Dickory, Dock

Hickory, dickory, dock!
The mouse ran up the clock.
The clock struck one,
The mouse ran down,
Hickory, dickory, dock.

Little Bo Peep

Little Bo Peep has lost her sheep,
And doesn't know where to find them.
Leave them alone, and they'll
    come home
Wagging their tails behind them!

Do You Know the Muffin Man?

Do you know the muffin man,
The muffin man, the muffin man?
Do you know the muffin man,
Who lives on Drury Lane?
Yes, I know the muffin man,
The muffin man, the muffin man.
Yes, I know the muffin man,
Who lives on Drury Lane.

Little Miss Muffet

Little Miss Muffet
Sat on her tuffet
Eating her curds and whey.
Along came a spider,
Who sat down beside her,
And frightened Miss Muffet away.

Jack and Jill

Jack and Jill went up a hill
To fetch a pail of water.
Jack fell down and broke his crown
And Jill came tumbling after.

Jack Be Nimble

Jack be nimble. Jack be quick.
Jack jump over the candlestick.

Humpty Dumpty

Humpty Dumpty sat on a wall.
Humpty Dumpty had a great fall.
All the king's horses and all the
    king's men
Could not put Humpty together
again.

Bo Peep has found her sheep!

Materials

- pattern on page 50
- photocopies of children's pictures
- small paper plates
- white cotton balls

- white and black construction paper
- transparency
- overhead projector
- green craft paper

- border
- markers and crayons
- glue
- scissors
- stapler

Directions

Teacher Preparation: Duplicate the sheep head pattern on white construction paper so that each child will have one. Find a picture of Bo Peep that you like and copy it. Then make a transparency of Bo Peep. Cover the board with the craft paper. Use an overhead projector to enlarge and copy Bo Peep on the bulletin board. Color Bo Peep. Finally add a festive border and the caption. Provide each child with a photocopy of his or her picture.

1. Glue cotton balls on the back of a paper plate to make a sheep's body.

2. Cut out a sheep head.

3. Glue your photo on the sheep head.

4. Glue the head on the body.

Help children staple their sheep to the bulletin board.

Nursery Rhyme Centers

Language Center

Language Arts Standard
Knows the alphabetical order of letters

Old MacDonald's ABC

Materials

- activity master on page 51
- alphabet line
- crayons

Teacher Preparation: Duplicate the activity master for each child.

Lead children in singing "The ABC Song" as you point to the letters on the line. Explain that children will connect the dots of capital letters to find a mystery picture. Then have children connect the dots from A to Z and color the picture.

Math Center

Math Standard
Places objects or events in order

Miss Muffet Order

Materials

- activity master on page 52
- crayons

Teacher Preparation: Duplicate the activity master for each child.

Lead children in reciting the rhyme "Little Miss Muffet." Then have them write 1, 2, or 3 to show the order of events.

Nursery Rhyme Centers

Sensory Center

Math Standard
Applies and adopts a variety of appropriate strategies to solve problems

Muffin Man Muffins

Materials

- mixing bowl
- kitchen tongs
- cotton balls
- muffin pan

Teacher Preparation: Fill the mixing bowl with the cotton balls.

Review the "Do You Know the Muffin Man?" rhyme. Then invite children to use the tongs to fill the muffin pan with cotton ball "muffins."

Science Center

Science Standard
Collects data gained from experiments

Jack and Jill's Pail

Materials

- pail
- sentence strip
- water
- crayons
- a variety of objects that float (sponge, ping-pong ball, leaf, crayon, etc.)
- a variety of objects that sink (paper clip, penny, metal spoon, etc)
- paper

Teacher Preparation: Fill the pail with water. Cut a sentence strip in half. Label one half "float" and one half "sink." Fold paper in half.

Lead students in reciting the rhyme "Jack and Jill." Then explain that Jack and Jill let you borrow their pail for an experiment. Show children the word signs. Invite them to guess which items will float, or stay on top of the water, and which items will sink, or fall to the bottom of the pail. Ask them to sort the items into groups. Then have them test their guesses. When children are done, have them write the name of each object on one half of a sheet of paper and draw pictures of the results.

Nursery Rhyme Centers

 ## Writing Center

Language Arts Standard
Writes words that move left to right

Feeling Scared

Materials

• activity master on page 53
• crayons

Teacher Preparation: Duplicate the activity master for each child.

Recite the "Little Miss Muffet" rhyme. Then read aloud the sentence frame. Help children complete the sentence frame and have them draw a picture to go with it.

 ## Block Center

Math Standard
Counts to 10

Jack Jumps

Materials

• blocks
• ruler

Review the rhyme "Jack Be Nimble." Then invite children to take turns stacking blocks to heights no taller than the ruler. Have them count the number of blocks, repeat the rhyme, and jump over the block "candlesticks."

Nursery Rhyme Centers

Dramatic Play Center

Social Studies Standard
Creates and interprets visuals including pictures and maps

Rhyme Repeat

Materials

- rhyme props, such as bowl, spoon, spider, candlestick, mittens, muffin pan, farm, stuffed animals

Teacher Preparation: Scatter the props around the center.

Ask children to choose a prop and use it to role-play a rhyme as others watch.

Game Center

Language Arts Standard
Listens to and responds to a variety of literature

Go Togethers

Materials

- picture cards on page 54
- markers
- white construction paper
- scissors

Teacher Preparation: Duplicate the picture cards on construction paper. Color and cut apart the cards.

Review the picture names. Then invite the children to pair the pictures that belong in the same nursery rhyme.

Clock and Mouse Patterns

Use with "Hickory, Dickory, Clock" on page 41.

slit line

12 11 1 10 2 9 3 8 4 7 5 6

mouse

clock

Mitten Pattern

Use with "Kitten Mitten" on page 41.

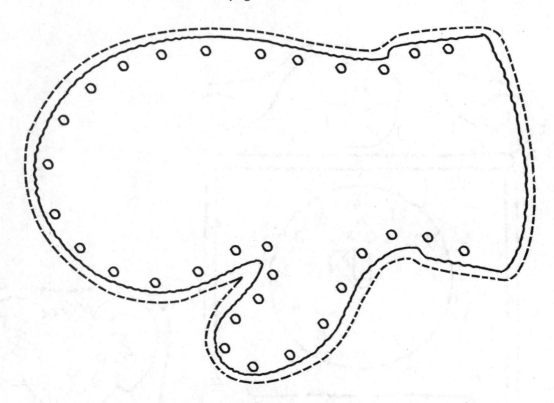

Sheep Head Pattern

Use with "Bo Peep Has Found Her Sheep!" on page 44.

Name _____

Old MacDonald's Farm

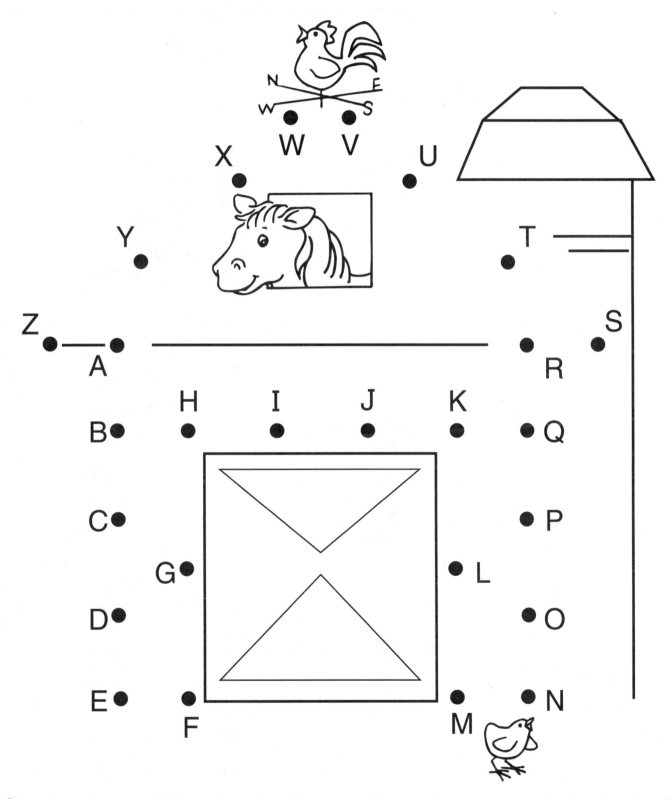

Directions: Use with "Old MacDonald's ABC" on page 45. Have children connect the dots from A to Z and color the picture.

51

Unit 4, A Visit with Mother Goose: Activity Master
Three Cheers for September PreK–K, SV 9828-0

Name _____

First, Next, Last

Directions: Use with "Miss Muffet Order" on page 45. Have children write *1*, *2*, or *3* to show the order of events.

Name _____

Just Like Miss Muffet

I get scared when

_____

_ _ _ _ _ _ _ _ _ _ _ _ _ _ _ _ _ _ _

_____.

Directions: Use with "Feeling Scared" on page 47. Help children complete the sentence frame and have them draw a picture to go with it.

Nursery Rhyme Picture Cards

Use with "Go Togethers" on page 48.

Unit 4, A Visit with Mother Goose: Cards
Three Cheers for September PreK–K, SV 9828-0

Community News

 The pants that firefighters wear are called "turnouts" because they are turned inside out with the boots attached when firefighters are not using them. The clothing firefighters wear is made of a special material that will not catch on fire.

 The first mail in America was delivered by ship captains. The mail was collected in bags that hung in taverns. The captain picked up the mail and would give it to people when the ship stopped in the different ports.

 From April 1860 to October 1861, men rode horses across America to carry mail between the coasts. They rode about 75 to 100 miles a day, changing horses every 10 to 15 miles. Mail took from 7 to 10 days to cross the country.

 Nearly 2,500 jobs in construction and related industries are generated when 1,000 houses are built.

 The first salespeople did not work in shops. They carried their goods in sacks and walked from village to village, selling or trading with the people living there.

 The very first hammers were made by prehistoric men and women. They tied rocks to wooden handles using vines or strips of animal hide.

 Some machines used to build roads include the:

- milling machine, which scrapes up to eight inches off the top of a road;
- concrete truck, which carries the stone and water to make some surfaces;
- gravel spreader, which spreads the small pea-size rock to cover tar;
- striping machine, which can paint up to 20 miles of lines on a road.

 In 1995, the Wheat Montana Farms and Bakery earned the Guinness World Record for the fastest baking of a loaf of bread. Workers harvested wheat from the field and milled it. Then they made bread dough and baked a loaf—all in 8 minutes, 13 seconds.

55

Unit 5, Helpers in Our Neighborhood: Teacher Information
Three Cheers for September PreK–K, SV 9828-0

Doctor's Kit

Materials

- patterns on page 64
- 13 x 9 black construction paper
- cotton balls
- adhesive bandages
- tongue depressors
- gauze bandages
- crayons
- scissors
- glue

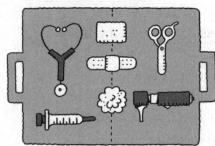

Directions

Teacher Preparation: Duplicate a set of the doctor's tools for each child. Fold a sheet of black construction paper in half for each child and cut the top, open sides to look like briefcase handles of a doctor's kit.

1. Color and cut out the doctor's tools.

2. Glue the tools on the inside of the kit.

3. Glue a cotton ball, adhesive bandage, tongue depressor, and a gauze bandage inside the kit, too.

4. Leave the kit open to dry.

Police Badge

Materials

- patterns on page 64
- poster board
- large paper clip
- foil
- scissors
- glue

Directions

Teacher Preparation: Cut out the badge pattern and trace one on poster board for each child. Duplicate a word patch and star symbol for each child. Cut the foil into squares.

1. Push a paper clip over the top, flat part of a poster board badge.

2. Cover one side of the badge with foil, leaving the other side uncovered so that the paper clip shows.

3. Color and cut out a word patch and a star symbol.

4. Glue the patch and symbol on the front of the badge.

5. When the badge is dry, clip the patch on your shirt.

Firefighter Ladder and Hose

You will need

- six-inch pretzel sticks
- small pretzel sticks
- spreadable cream cheese
- red licorice strings
- large paper plates

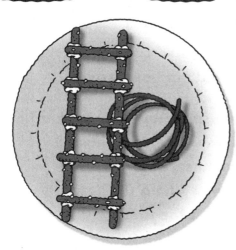

Directions

1. To make the long sides of the ladder, lay two six-inch pretzel sticks on a plate so they are about two inches apart.

2. Get five small pretzels to make the rungs of the ladder.

3. Dip each end of the small pretzel sticks in the cream cheese. Lay them perpendicular on the long pretzels.

4. To make the firefighter hose, get one string of licorice.

5. Wrap the licorice around two fingers to make a coil.

6. Lay the hose beside the ladder.

Note: Be aware of children who may have food allergies.

Neighborly Books

The Berenstain Bears on the Job
by Stan and Jan Berenstain
(Random House Trade)

Community Helpers from A to Z
by Bobbie Kalman and Niki Walker
(Crabtree Publishing)

Curious George Takes a Job
by H. A. Rey (Houghton Mifflin)

Fox on the Job
by James Marshall (Puffin Book)

Jobs Around My Neighborhood/Oficios en Mi Vecindario
by Gladys Rosa-Mendoza (Me + Mi Publishing)

Jobs People Do
by Christopher Maynard (DK Publishing)

Officer Buckle and Gloria
by Peggy Rathmann (Putnam Publishing)

What Will I Be?
by Phoebe Beinstein (Simon Spotlight/ Nickelodeon)

♫ Let's All Look
(Tune: "Here We Go 'Round the Mulberry Bush")

Teacher Preparation: Duplicate the job cards on pages 68 and 69. Hold the correct card up as the class sings or invite a volunteer to find the matching card after singing each verse. The first verse does not have a job card.

(Place a hand over the eyes and look around.)
Let's all look at many jobs,
  many jobs, many jobs.
Let's all look at many jobs,
  all around (name of your city).

(Look in someone's ear with a pretend otoscope.)
This is the way I check your ears,
  check your ears, check your ears.
This is the way I check your ears,
  when you pay me a visit.

(Pantomime kneading dough.)
This is the way I make your bread,
  make your bread, make your bread.
This is the way I make your bread,
  before it comes to your store.

(Pantomime hammering.)
This is the way I fix the house,
  fix the house, fix the house.
This is the way I fix the house,
  if something there is broken.

(Spread arms out to the side and "fly" around.)
This is the way I fly the plane,
  fly the plane, fly the plane.
This is the way I fly the plane,
  So you get where you're going.

(Pantomime sorting letters.)
This is the way I sort the mail,
  sort the mail, sort the mail.
This is the way I sort the mail,
  so you will get your letters.

(Pantomime spraying water with a hose.)
This is the way I hold the hose,
  hold the hose, hold the hose,
This is the way I hold the hose,
  so I put out the fire.

(Pantomime pointing to a weather map.)
This is the way I talk on TV,
  talk on TV, talk on TV.
This is the way I talk on TV
  so you will know the weather.

(Pantomime opening books and stamping.)
This is the way I stamp the books,
  stamp the books, stamp the books.
This is the way I stamp the books
  so you can read at home.

Three Cheers for September PreK–K, SV 9828-0

Materials

- white construction paper
- crayons
- marker
- craft paper
- border
- scissors
- stapler

Directions

Teacher Preparation: Cover the board with the craft paper. Add a festive border and the caption. Discuss with children jobs they would like to do when they grow up and why they would like to do these jobs.

1. Draw a picture of a community helper you would like to be someday.

2. Write or dictate a sentence to go along with the picture.

Invite children to share their ideas during circle time. Then help them staple their pictures to the bulletin board.

Career Centers

Math Center

Math Standard
Counts sets of objects

Tooth Count

Materials

- patterns on page 65
- envelopes
- file folders
- scissors
- white construction paper
- markers
- large paper clips
- glue

Teacher Preparation: Duplicate ten toothbrushes and fifty-five teeth on construction paper for each file folder game that you plan to make. Color the toothbrushes and write numbers 1 through 10 on the handles. Cut out the toothbrushes and teeth. Glue the toothbrushes on the folders, placing five on each side in numerical order. Place all the teeth in an envelope and clip it to the folder.

Lead children in a discussion of dentists and the jobs they do. Then invite children to look at the numeral on each toothbrush and count out the corresponding number of teeth.

Language Center

Language Arts Standard
Recognizes uppercase and lowercase letters

Mail Matchup

Materials

- envelopes
- index cards
- marker

Teacher Preparation: Write capital letters on separate envelopes and lowercase letters on index cards.

Have children place the lowercase letters into the matching capital-letter envelopes.

Extension: For a phonemic awareness activity, draw or cut out pairs of pictures whose names have the same beginning sounds. For example, cut out pictures of a fox and a fan. Glue one on an envelope and the other on an index card. Children make a match by listening for the beginning /f/ sound.

Career Centers

Dramatic Play Center

Social Studies Standard
Understands the importance of jobs

Bakery Fun

Materials

- play dough
- aprons
- poster board
- marker
- cookie cutters
- rolling pins, plastic knives, pancake turners
- cookie trays, pie plates, cake rounds, muffin tins

Teacher Preparation: Make a "Bakery" sign on the poster board and hang it in the center.

Discuss with children the people who prepare food, including bakers, restaurant cooks, and school cooks. Discuss why these people are important community helpers. Then invite children to make play dough bakery treats, including cookies, pies, cakes, and muffins, to sell. Then have them take turns role-playing the baker and customers.

Sensory Center

Language Arts Standard
Knows the values of a penny, nickel, and dime

Clerk Work

Materials

- cards on page 66
- play money
- cash box
- tub

Teacher Preparation: Duplicate, color, and cut out the coin cards. Tape one on the bottom of each section of the cash box. Fill the tub with the play money.

Discuss the job that store clerks and cashiers do. Ask children where they see people who have these kinds of jobs. Then display and name the four different coins. Discuss the value of each coin. Have children sort the play money in the appropriate sections of the "cash box" and say the value of each coin.

Note: Craft stores sell inexpensive plastic boxes with moveable dividers. These work well as cash boxes.

Career Centers

Reading Center

Math Standard
Sorts or classifies by size, color, shape, or kind

Like a Librarian

Materials

- fiction books about animals, sports, jobs, transportation
- construction paper
- stamps
- scissors
- large basket
- nonfiction books about animals, sports, jobs, transportation
- marker
- inkpads
- small basket

Teacher Preparation: Cut the construction paper into strips for "library cards" for the books. Write the name of each book on a card and place it in the book so it sticks out. Set up the center with a desk, chair, inkpad, and stamp. The small basket will hold the cards when books are "checked out," and the large basket is for returned books.

Lead children in a discussion about their visits to a library and the tasks that a librarian performs. If possible, arrange a visit to the school or local library so the librarian can talk with the children. Then have children role-play being in a library. They can take turns being the librarians who help find books for visitors and check out the books by stamping the cards. They can also match the card to the book when it is returned and sort the books by genre or by topic. Challenge librarians to have a story time for visitors to their library.

Block Center

Math Standard
Uses familiar manipulatives to recognize shapes and their relationships

Road Crew Roads

Materials

- a variety of toy trucks large enough to carry blocks or that are involved in construction
- toy cars

Have children use the vehicles and blocks to build roads.

Career Centers

Puzzle Center

Science Standard
Understands properties and characteristics of objects

Builder's Tools

Materials

- toolbox or shoe box
- tools (hammer, wrench, screw driver, ruler, pliers, and other tools that are not sharp)
- craft paper
- permanent marker

Teacher Preparation: Lay the tools on the craft paper, spacing them out. Then trace around each tool. Put all the tools into a toolbox or shoe box on the table for storage.

Help children name each tool as it is displayed and talk about how it is used. Discuss the jobs people do that might require the tools. Then invite children to match the tools to their outlines as you display each one.

Science Center

Social Studies Standard
Describe the weather and how it affects us

What to Wear, Weather Forecaster?

Materials

- activity master on page 67
- blank video
- crayons
- television

Teacher Preparation: Duplicate the activity master for each child. Record a videotape of a weather forecaster from a television newscast.

Play the weather videotape for children. Discuss the job that a weather forecaster does and why it is helpful to know about the weather in advance. Then have children draw lines to correctly match the clothes with the weather.

Doctor's Tools Patterns

Use with "Doctor's Kit" on page 56.

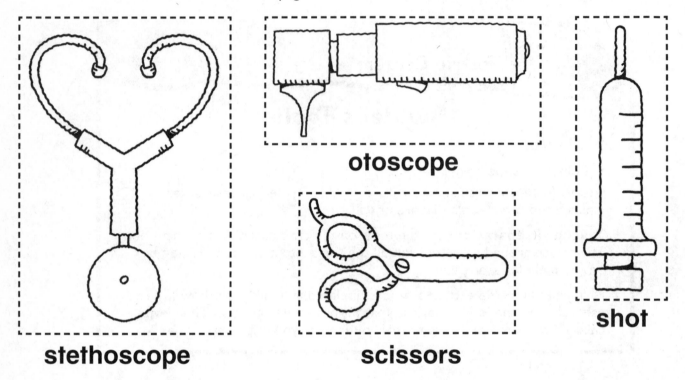

stethoscope

otoscope

scissors

shot

Police Badge Patterns

Use with "Police Badge" on page 56.

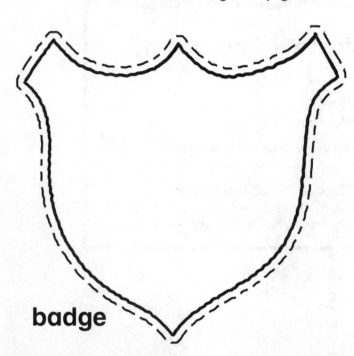

badge

patch

star symbol

Toothbrush and Tooth Patterns

Use with "Tooth Count" on page 60.

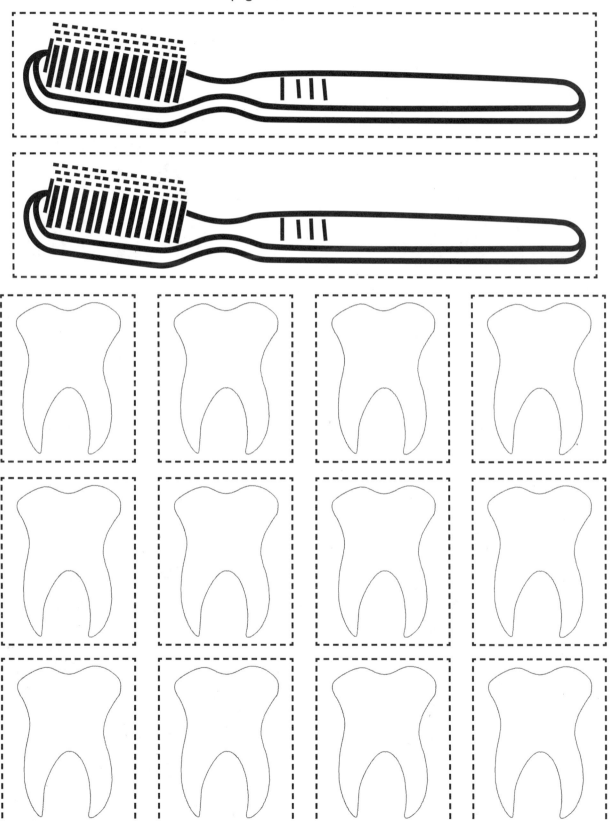

Three Cheers for September PreK–K, SV 9828-0

Cash Box Coin Cards

Use with "Clerk Work" on page 61.

penny

dime

nickel

quarter

Name _____

Dress for the Weather

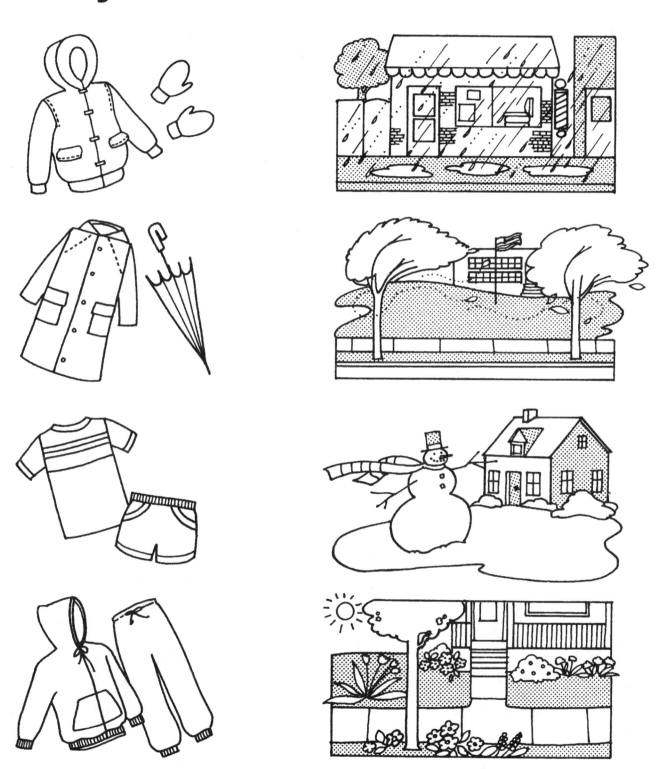

Directions: Use with "What to Wear, Weather Forecaster?" on page 63. Have children draw lines to match the clothes with the weather.

Three Cheers for September PreK–K, SV 9828-0

Job Cards

Use with the song "Let's All Look" on page 58.

doctor

baker

carpenter

pilot

Job Cards

Use with the song "Let's All Look" on page 58.

mail carrier

firefighter

weather forecaster

librarian

Apple Facts

 Apples are part of the rose family.

 The state of Washington grows the most apples in the United States.

 There are over 7,500 different kinds of apples in the world.

 Apples have five seeds.

 An apple cut in half across its core will have a symmetrical star shape.

 The freshest apples can float because 25 percent of their volume is air.

 One tree can produce enough apples to fill 20 boxes that weigh nearly 42 pounds each. That's 20 bushels of apples!

 John Chapman became known as Johnny Appleseed. He spent nearly 49 years walking around Ohio and Indiana planting and caring for apple orchards.

 The largest apple ever picked weighed over three pounds.

 It takes two pounds of apples to make one nine-inch apple pie.

 A bushel of apples will produce 20–24 quarts of applesauce.

 It takes 36 apples to make one gallon of cider.

 On October 16, 1976, Kathy Wafler Madison, at the age of 16, created the world's longest apple peel. It was 172 feet, 4 inches long. Madison later worked as a sales manager for an apple tree nursery.

Three Cheers for September PreK–K, SV 9828-0

Inside, Outside Apples

Materials

- patterns on page 79
- small paper plates
- apple seeds
- paintbrushes
- green and brown construction paper
- red tempera paint
- glue
- scissors
- hole punch
- string or yarn

Directions

Teacher Preparation: In advance, save and dry seeds from apples. Trace and cut out a brown stem and a green leaf for each child. Cut yarn into 18-inch lengths.

1. Paint the backside of a paper plate red for the outside of an apple. Set it aside to dry.

2. Glue a brown stem and a green leaf to the red apple.

3. Glue apple seeds in the center of the white side of the plate to show the inside of an apple.

4. Punch a hole near the top of the apple.

5. Thread yarn through the hole and tie the apple on one end of the yarn.

6. Hang the apple from the ceiling.

Apple Orchard

Materials

- pattern on page 79
- green felt
- craft sticks
- green construction paper
- red tempera paint
- brown markers
- clean meat trays
- wet and dry paper towels
- scissors
- glue
- clay

Directions

Teacher Preparation: Trace and cut out two treetops from the green paper for each child. Fold and place a dry paper towel in a meat tray. Pour red paint over the paper towel to make a stamp pad. When the trees are dry, lay out a piece of green felt. Invite children to "plant" their trees in the "apple orchard."

1. Lay two treetops on a table.

2. Press a finger in the red paint. Make prints on the treetops to look like apples. Set aside to dry.

3. Use a brown marker to color a craft stick for a tree trunk.

4. Glue one treetop to the trunk so that the apples can be seen.

5. Matching the treetop edges, glue another treetop to the other side of the trunk, making sure the apples can be seen on this side, too.

6. Roll clay into a ball to make a stand.

7. Push the trunk into the clay so that the apple tree stands.

Baked Apples

You will need

- apples
- raisins
- brown sugar
- ground cinnamon
- apple juice
- knife
- cutting board
- electric skillet
- measuring spoons
- vegetable cooking spray

Directions

Teacher Preparation: Cut apples in half and core them. Spray a skillet and heat it to 350°F. Bake the prepared apples for 15–20 minutes or until they are soft.

1. Place an apple with the cut side up on a plate.

2. Put six raisins in the hole of the apple.

3. Sprinkle one teaspoon of brown sugar over the raisins.

4. Sprinkle one-fourth teaspoon of cinnamon over the sugar.

5. Pour one tablespoon of apple juice over the entire apple.

6. Ask an adult to bake the apples in the skillet.

Note: Be aware of children who may have food allergies.

♫ Apple, Apple on the Tree

(Tune: "Twinkle, Twinkle, Little Star")

Apple, apple on the tree

You will taste so good to me.

Shall I bake you in a pie?

Warm and sweet, I think I'll try.

Apple, apple on the tree,

Apple pie is so YUMMY!

Apple, apple on the tree

You will taste so good to me.

Apple juice is never sour,

I could drink it every hour.

Apple, apple on the tree,

Apple juice is right for me!

Apple, apple on the tree

You will taste so good to me.

With a meal or as a snack

Applesauce makes my lips smack.

Apple, apple on the tree,

Applesauce fills me with glee!

Books Worth Biting Into . . .

Apples
by Gail Gibbons (Holiday House)

Apples, Apples, Apples
by Nancy Elizabeth Wallace (Winslow Press)

How Do Apples Grow?
by Betsy Maestro and Giulio Maestro
(HarperTrophy)

How to Make an Apple Pie and See the World
by Marjorie Priceman (Knopf)

Johnny Appleseed
by Steven Kellogg (Scholastic)

The Seasons of Arnold's Apple Tree
by Gail Gibbons (Harcourt Brace
and Jovanovich)

Ten Apples Up on Top!
by Theo Le Sieg (Random House)

Ten Red Apples
by Pat Hutchins (Greenwillow)

Apples of My Eye

Materials

- patterns on page 79
- pattern on page 80
- copies of children's pictures
- old file folders
- tempera paints

- red, green, yellow, and brown construction paper
- craft paper
- overhead projector
- transparency

- border
- paintbrushes
- scissors
- glue
- stapler

Directions

Teacher Preparation: Cover the board with the craft paper. Make a transparency of the tree pattern. Use the transparency to trace a large tree in the center of the bulletin board. Paint the tree. Trace several apple, stem, and leaf patterns on the folders and cut them out. Cut the red, brown, and green paper into squares close in size to the patterns. Cut out apple shapes from red, yellow, and green paper to make a patterned border. Begin a repeated pattern with the apples across the top of the bulletin board. Add the caption.

1. Trace an apple on a red square. Cut it out.

2. Trace a stem on a brown square. Cut it out.

3. Trace a leaf on a green square. Cut it out.

4. Glue the parts of the apple together.

5. Glue your picture on the apple.

Help children staple their apples to the bulletin board in a pleasing arrangement. Then have them choose the color of apple that comes next in the border pattern. Help them staple it to the board.

Orchard Centers

Language Center

Language Arts Standard
Identifies beginning sounds

Apple Sounds

Materials

- activity master on page 82
- crayons or markers

Teacher Preparation: Duplicate the activity master for each child.

Explain that *apple* begins with /a/. Have children color the pictures whose names begin with the same sound as *apple*.

Math Center

Math Standard
Compares groups and recognizes more than, less than, and equal to

Apple Counting

Materials

- pattern on page 80
- white construction paper
- number cube
- cards on page 81
- markers
- scissors

Teacher Preparation: Duplicate two tree patterns and the apple counters on construction paper. Color the trees and apples. Cut apart the counters.

Give each partner a tree. Ask partners to take turns rolling the cube. Have them count out the number of apples shown on the cube to put on their tree. Have children discuss which tree has more apples, less apples, or equal amounts of apples after each person has rolled the cube once, twice, and so on.

Orchard Centers

Sensory Center

Science Standard
Observes and describes properties of objects

Apple Sort

Materials

- several each of red, yellow, green, and mixed apples
- large apple basket
- smaller baskets

Teacher Preparation: Put all the apples into one large basket.

Have children sort the apples by color.

Reading Center

Language Arts Standard
Distinguishes different forms of text

"Apple" Is the Word

Materials

- food labels and ads that contain the word *apple*
- belted rain jackets
- hand lenses
- tape

Teacher Preparation: Tape the labels and ads on the wall.

Invite children to pretend that they are detectives. Have them find the word *apple* on each label and in each ad.

Orchard Centers

Science Center

Science Standard
Observes, compares, and describes properties and parts of plants

Apple Parts

Materials

- pattern on page 81
- apple
- drawing paper
- knife
- poster board
- lemon juice
- markers and crayons
- tape

Teacher Preparation: Enlarge the apple parts pattern and draw it on poster board. Then color and label the diagram. Tape the poster on a wall in the science center. Cut an apple in half and sprinkle lemon juice on it. You will need to change the apple daily.

Have children use the poster to identify each part on the fresh apple. Then have them draw and label their own apple.

Writing Center

Language Arts Standard
Uses letters to represent words

Apple Tree Seasons

Materials

- booklet on pages 83 and 84
- stapler
- crayons or markers
- construction paper
- pencils

Teacher Preparation: Duplicate the booklet pages. Make a cover from construction paper and assemble the booklets. Provide a copy for each child. Before introducing the center, read aloud *The Seasons of Arnold's Apple Tree* by Gail Gibbons.

Lead children in a discussion of the four seasons. Then remind children of how an apple tree looks in each season. Invite children to make a booklet that tells about an apple tree. Read aloud the sentences on the booklet pages as children follow along. Have them trace each word and color the pictures. On the last page, ask children to draw lots of apples on the ground on the last page. You may wish to invite them to include themselves picking an apple, too.

Orchard Centers

Dramatic Play Center

Language Arts Standard
Begins to use speaking and listening, in a group and with support, to define and solve problems

Apple Pie Bakery

Materials

- play dough
- flat baking trays
- apple-shaped cookie cutters
- foil pie plates
- rolling pins
- aprons
- poster board
- markers

Teacher Preparation: Make a sign that says "Apple Pie Bakery." Arrange the center like a kitchen in a bakery.

Invite children to role-play bakers. They can take turns cutting apple shapes out of flattened dough with the cookie cutters, rolling out the pie crust, and assembling the pie to bake.

Game Center

Math Standard
Reads numbers to 10

Apple Hop

Materials

- patterns on page 79
- glue
- scissors
- red, yellow, and green construction paper
- tape
- marker

Teacher Preparation: Enlarge the apple pattern so that it is the size of a sheet of construction paper. Enlarge the stem and leaf patterns to the same proportion as the apple. Duplicate the apple pattern on five pieces each of red, green, and yellow paper. Duplicate 15 brown stems and 15 green leaves. Cut out all pieces and assemble the apples. Write the numbers 1 through 5 on each color set of apples. Finally, mix the apples together and tape them on the floor, making sure that children can easily jump to each color set in numerical order.

Have children take turns choosing a color and jumping to the apples. They can jump forwards or backwards in numerical order. Encourage them to say the number names before jumping. Challenge children to jump to apples that have the same number but are of different colors.

Apple Pieces Patterns

Use with "Inside, Outside Apples" on page 71, "Apple Orchard" on page 71, "Apples of My Eye" on page 74, and "Apple Hop" on page 78.

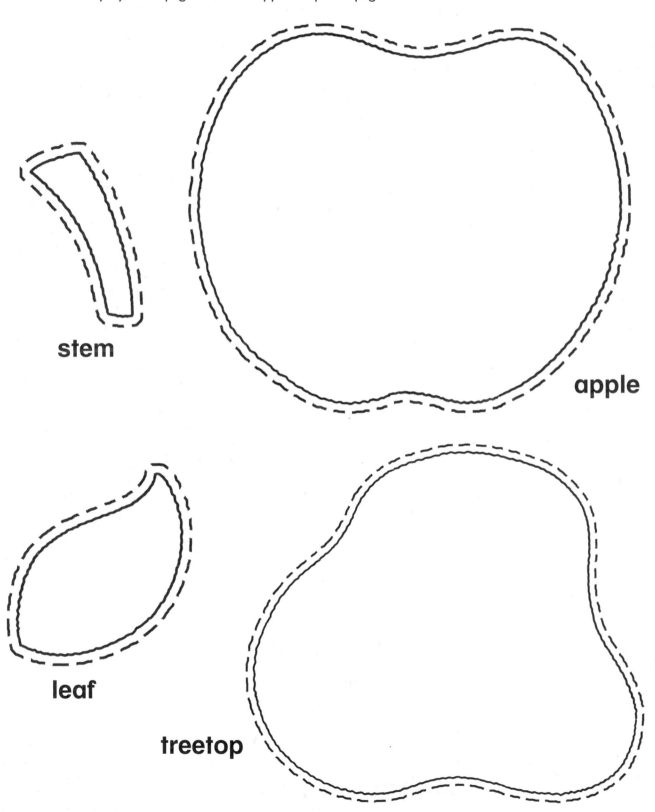

stem

apple

leaf

treetop

Three Cheers for September PreK–K, SV 9828-0

Apple Tree Pattern

Use with "Apples of My Eye" on page 74 and "Apple Counting" on page 75.

Apple Counter Cards

Use with "Apple Counting" on page 75.

Apple Parts Pattern

Use with "Apple Parts" on page 77.

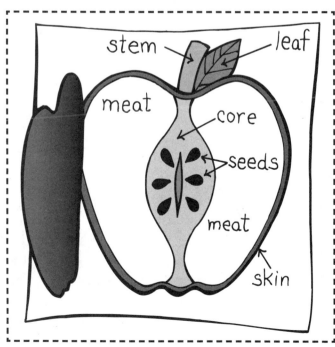

stem   leaf
meat   core
        seeds
meat
skin

Unit 6, Apples, Apples, Apples: Cards/Pattern
Three Cheers for September PreK–K, SV 9828-0

Name _____

Beginning Sounds

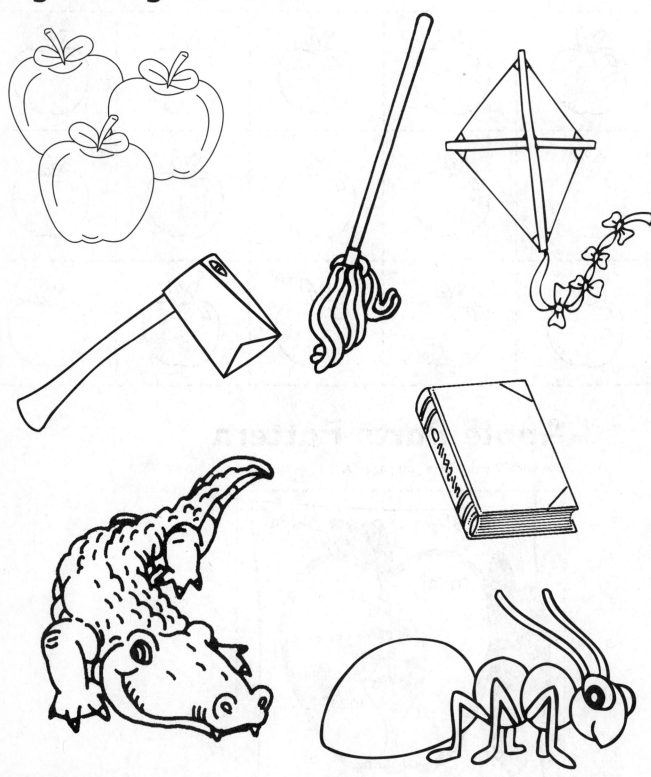

Directions: Use with "Apple Sounds" on page 75. Explain that *apple* begins with /a/. Have children color the pictures whose names begin with the same sound as *apple*.

82

Unit 6, Apples, Apples, Apples: Activity Master
Three Cheers for September PreK–K, SV 9828-0

The Apple Tree Booklet

Use with "Apple Tree Seasons" on page 77.

This is the _____ apple _____ tree in winter.

1

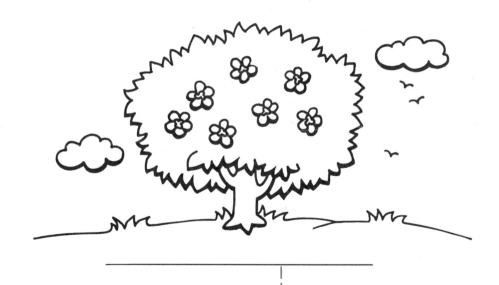

This is the _____ apple _____ tree in spring.

2

www.harcourtschoolsupply.com
© Harcourt Achieve Inc. All rights reserved.

Unit 6, Apples, Apples, Apples: Activity Master
Three Cheers for September PreK–K, SV 9828-0

The Apple Tree Booklet

Use with "Apple Tree Seasons" on page 77.

This is the _____ apple _____ tree in summer.

3

This is the _____ apple _____ tree in fall.

4

Unit 6, Apples, Apples, Apples: Activity Master
Three Cheers for September PreK–K, SV 9828-0

A Look at Tomie dePaola

 Tomie dePaola, a well-known children's author and illustrator, was born September 15, 1934, in Meriden, Connecticut. He lived with his mother, father, brother, and two sisters.

 Tomie knew that he wanted to write and illustrate books beginning at the age of four. He also wanted to tap dance; he still enjoys tap-dancing today.

 While growing up, Tomie took art and dance classes.

 Tomie went to art school after graduating from high school.

 He taught art from 1962 to 1978 at various schools and colleges.

 Tomie now lives in New Hampshire and has two Welsh terrier dogs that keep him company. Their names are Markus and Moffat.

 Popcorn is Tomie's favorite food. He even wrote a book about it called *The Popcorn Book* (Holiday House).

 He has illustrated over 200 books in his 40 years in the publishing business. Of those books, he has written more than 100 of them.

 Tomie has won awards for many of his books, including a Caldecott Honor Award (*Strega Nona*), a Newbery Honor Award (*26 Fairmont Avenue*), and the New Hampshire Governor's Arts of Living Treasure.

 26 Fairmont Avenue (the series), *The Art Lesson*, and *Nana Upstairs & Nana Downstairs* are books that Tomie wrote about himself.

 The heart is a special symbol for Tomie, so he draws it in all of his books.

 Tomie has a distinct folk art style.

Three Cheers for September PreK–K, SV 9828-0

The Legend of the Bluebonnet
by Tomie dePaola (PaperStar Books)

Tell children that a legend is a very old story that has a hero. Invite children to listen to *The Legend of the Bluebonnet* to find out who the hero is and what the hero does. Have children do the following activities.

Popcorn Bluebonnet

Materials: pattern on page 89, dry blue tempera paint, 2 large plastic bowls, popped popcorn, green markers, glue, white construction paper, plastic container with a lid, slotted spoon

Directions

Teacher Preparation: Duplicate the pattern for each child. Put dry paint into a container. Drop half of the popcorn into the container, cover it, and shake. Scoop popcorn out, shaking off excess paint, and put popcorn in a large bowl. Put white popcorn in the other bowl.

Invite children to color the stem and leaves green. Have them glue blue and white popcorn along the top of the stem to make a bluebonnet flower.

Indian Doll

Materials: pattern on page 90, crayons, white and brown construction paper, blue craft feathers, glue, scissors

Directions

Teacher Preparation: Duplicate the doll pattern for each child. Cut brown rectangles that are 1" x 4".

Invite children to make the doll in the story. Have them color the doll. Then show them how to cut one edge of two brown rectangles into strips to make fringe for the pants. Have them glue the uncut sides of the rectangles to the pants. Then have them glue two feathers in the doll's hair.

I Was Brave

Materials: activity master on page 91, crayons

Directions

Teacher Preparation: Duplicate the activity master for each child.

Remind children that the girl in the story was very brave when she gave up her most loved possession. Invite children to draw a picture and dictate a sentence about a time when they were brave.

Books by Tomie dePaola

- *26 Fairmont Avenue* (Putnam)

- *The Art Lesson* (Putnam)

- *Bill and Pete* (Putnam)

- *The Comic Adventures of Old Mother Hubbard and Her Dog* (Voyager)

- *Hey Diddle Diddle & Other Mother Goose Rhymes* (Putnam)

- *The Legend of the Bluebonnet* (PaperStar Books)

- *The Legend of the Indian Paintbrush* (PaperStar Books)

- *Meet the Barkers* (Penguin Putnam)

- *Nana Upstairs & Nana Downstairs* (Putnam)

- *Strega Nona* (Simon & Schuster)

- *Tomie dePaola's Favorite Nursery Tales* (Putnam)

- *Tomie dePaola's Mother Goose* (Putnam)

- *Tomie dePaola's Mother Goose Favorites* (Grosset & Dunlap)

- *Tony's Bread* (Putnam)

- *What the Mailman Brought* (Putnam)

Bookmark Patterns

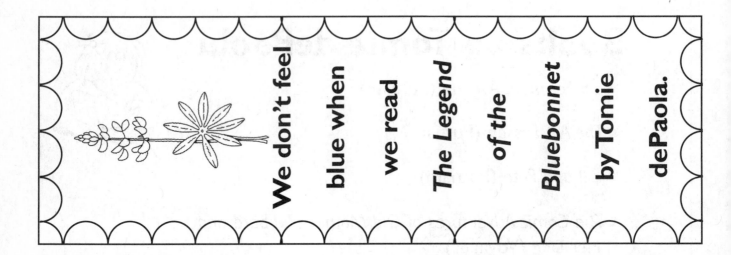

We don't feel blue when we read *The Legend of the Bluebonnet* by Tomie dePaola.

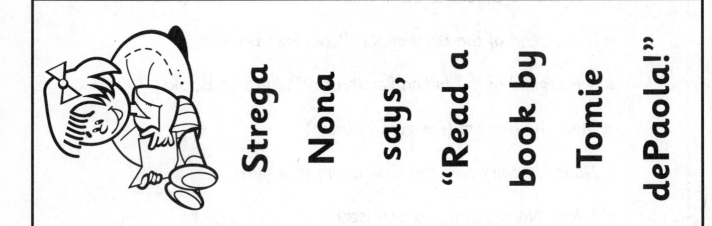

Strega Nona says, "Read a book by Tomie dePaola!"

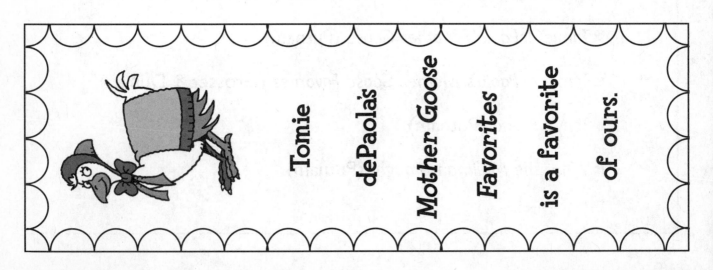

Tomie dePaola's *Mother Goose Favorites* is a favorite of ours.

Unit 7, Author Study: Patterns
Three Cheers for September PreK–K, SV 9828-0

Bluebonnet Pattern

Use with "Popcorn Bluebonnet" on page 86.

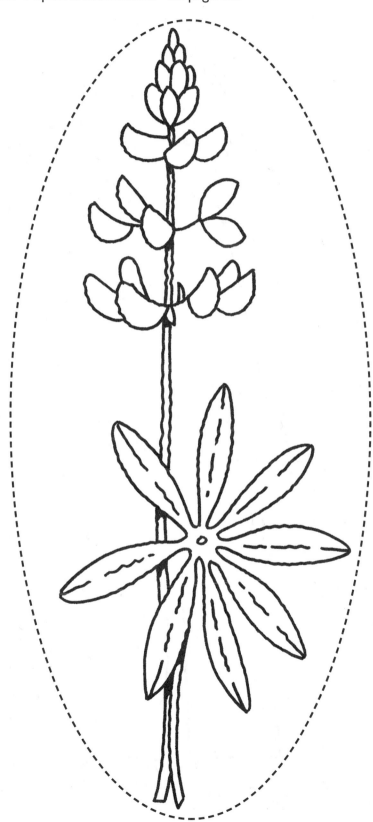

Doll Pattern

Use with "Indian Doll" on page 86.

Three Cheers for September PreK–K, SV 9828-0

Name _____

Feeling Brave

I was brave when I

_____

_____ .

Directions: Use with "I Was Brave" on page 86. Invite children to draw a picture to show a time when they were brave. Then have them dictate a sentence to tell about the picture.

91
Unit 7, Author Study: Activity Master
Three Cheers for September PreK–K, SV 9828-0

Center Icons Patterns

Art Center

Block Center

Dramatic Play Center

Game Center

Three Cheers for September PreK–K, SV 9828-0

Center Icons Patterns

Language Center

Math Center

Music Center

Puzzle Center

Center Icons Patterns

Reading Center

Science Center

Sensory Center

Writing Center